INDIANA

TO WASHINGTON

LITTLE PIGEON CREEK

OHIO RIVER

KENTUCKY

I.&E.P. d'AULAIRE

Published by Bantam Doubleday Dell Books for Young Readers, a division of
Bantam Doubleday Dell Publishing Group, Inc.
1540 Broadway, New York, New York 10036

ISBN: 0-440-40690-0

Reprinted by arrangement with Doubleday Books for Young Readers

Printed in the United States of America, February 1993,   10   9   8

ABRAHAM LINCOLN

by INGRI & EDGAR PARIN D'AULAIRE

A PICTURE YEARLING SPECIAL

Deep in the wilderness down in Kentucky there stood a cabin built of roughly hewn logs. It was a poor little cabin of only one room. The February wind tore at the clumsy door and made it rattle on its leather hinges. Just a glimmer of daylight sifted in through the oiled deer hide stretched across the single window frame. But the flames flickered gaily on the hearth. In this cabin lived a man named Thomas Lincoln with his wife and his little daughter, Sally. And here it was that his son, Abraham Lincoln, first saw the world on a Sunday morning. It wasn't much of a house in which he was born, but it was just as good as most people had in Kentucky in 1809.

"Abe is solemn like a little papoose," said the kinfolk who came to see him.

"He grows so fast I can't keep him in shirts," said his father.

His mother spun and sewed. Just as fast as he outgrew the old ones she had new little linsey shirts ready for him. And she played with him and watched him grow while the father was busy tilling the fields. Often she took Abe to a spring nearby and sat there in the shade singing little songs and psalms to him.

But the soil on the farm was meager, and the father grew tired of toiling with it. "I reckon we'll be moving," he said, and he bought a farm on Knob Creek on the other side of the hill. There Abe learned to help on the farm, even before he had his first pair of pants. He held the tools and he sat on the horse, and so Abe and his father and the horse plowed the fields together. And when planting time came his father strode in front, and Abe toddled behind him dropping seeds.

One day the father shot a buck in the woods, and from the skin the mother made Abe a pair of breeches. Abe stood beside her, watching every stitch she sewed. He felt very proud. Little children ran about in shirts and petticoats only, but now he would be a big boy in breeches. And Abe put on his buckskin breeches, washed his face and hands in the brook, and went off to school with his sister, Sally. The road to school was two miles long. On the way they met other children who came trotting down from the hills all about to the schoolhouse in the valley. There they sat together, big and small, reading and writing and reckoning aloud, all at one time together. There was such a chatter that it could be heard a long way off. But when Abe was six years old he had learned both to read and write. After that he didn't go much to school.

Abe lived down in the valley, and up on the hill lived a boy he played with often. Between the valley and the hill ran a brook, and across the brook there lay a log. The boys had to run over that log to get together to play. One day it had rained so hard that the brook ran fast, and the log across it was slippery. With a big splash Abe fell head first into the water. If his friend hadn't come running and fished him out with a pole, he would have drowned.

Abe's father didn't like to have neighbors too close by. "It is time to move when you see the smoke of your neighbor's chimney," he said one day when Abe was seven. "I reckon we'll be moving."

This time they traveled far, more than a hundred miles. They rode and they walked and they ferried until they left Kentucky and came to Indiana, the new state. There they borrowed a wagon and traveled on, right into the wilderness. The roads became narrower and rougher, the forest darker and denser. At last they stopped in the midst of the woods, at a place called Little Pigeon Creek. "Here we'll build our new home," said Abe's father.

While they were chopping down trees and building a shelter, the autumn sky and golden leaves were their roof. The shelter they built had only three walls, with an open hearth where the fourth wall should have been. Day and night they had to keep the fire burning. In a corner they put up a bed for the parents. On the ground

they spread bear skins over piles of dried leaves for Abe and Sally to sleep on. Then they unpacked the pots and pans and household goods, and settled down for the winter. And where Abe and his father had cut down the timber, they plowed and planted between the tree stumps.

That winter was long, but at last spring was there. Then the distant neighbors came to help them build a real cabin. It had four walls, but no window or door. They had to climb through a hole in the wall to get in and out. Up under the roof there was a loft where Abe was to sleep. Slowly the wilderness changed into a homestead. Often Abe and his family had only corn and potatoes to eat, but when hunting was good the father brought

game from the woods and Abe and Sally found berries and honey. And once in a long while the mother baked gingerbread. One day his mother gave Abe three gingerbread men all at once. He ran out under a tree to eat them slowly, all by himself. But hardly had he nibbled at the first one, when a fat little boy spotted him. "Abe, gimme a man," the little boy said. Abe gave him the larger one. The boy crammed the whole gingerbread into

his mouth, and before he had swallowed it he said: "Abe, gimme the other." And Abe gave him the other one, too, for he didn't know how to say no. "You seem to like gingerbread men," was all he said. "Abe," said the fat little boy, "nobody ever loved gingerbread as much as I do and gets so little of it." Slowly Abe ate his one gingerbread man, and wondered why the things he liked best were always the hardest to get.

He wanted to read and to study, but school was far away, and he had to stay at home to help on the farm. The hard work made him big and husky, and he could outrun and outwrestle all the other boys of his age. Even quicker than his legs ran his wit, so he became leader of all the boys who lived around Little Pigeon Creek. Abe hadn't much time to play, but sometimes at night he and his friends stole out to a salt lick in the woods. There they hid behind trees and watched the shy deer licking the salty slabs. But Abe never went hunting as other boys and menfolk did. He loved the animals and wouldn't harm them.

For two happy years Abe and his family lived in the home in the woods near wolves and grumbling bears. But when he was nine a dangerous sickness came to the wilderness, and his mother took sick and died. Then the woods seemed gloomy and dark, and the days grew long for Sally and Abe.

A year or so later their father went off on a trip, and for many weeks Abe and Sally were left all alone. Then one day a big wagon, drawn by four horses, stopped in front of the cabin. Out of the wagon jumped their father and a kind, rosy-cheeked woman. She ran over to Abe and Sally and hugged them to her bosom. She had come to be their new mother.

The stepmother had brought her three children, and all her household goods. They unloaded a chest, a table, chairs, and feather beds, pots and knives and forks and spoons. So smooth and fine was the furniture that Abe could run his hands over it without getting splinters in his fingers. And the stepmother climbed up to the loft where Abe slept. She threw out the leaves that had been his bedding, and gave him a soft feather bed instead. Then she put the father to work to make a real door, a window, and a wooden floor for the cabin. She washed and scrubbed the cabin both high and low, and took charge of the family right away.

"Let Abe have time to read," she said when she saw how eager to learn he was. At night, after the others had gone to sleep, she let him lie by the fireplace and study. In the flickering light he practised writing and reading. He wrote with charcoal on a wooden shovel, and read the Bible, stories about George Washington, "Pilgrim's Progress," and every other book he could get. Books were scarce in the wilderness, but Abe didn't mind walking twenty miles to borrow one.

When Abe grew too tired to read any more, he climbed up the pegs in the wall to his loft. Before going to sleep he hid the book he had been reading in a crack in the roof to keep it safe. But once a storm came up in the night, and when Abe woke up his book was soaking wet and spoiled. He had borrowed this book from a rich farmer, and for three long days Abe had to husk corn to pay for it. "No one can beat Abe Lincoln at farm work," said the neighbors. It was known for miles around how quick he was at splitting logs into fence rails. But when someone passed by, he would sit on the fence he had made and talk, asking questions to learn new things. Then the neighbors thought he was lazy. And when he walked between the handles of his plow reading a book, they thought he was queer.

Abe grew straight up into the air like a fir tree. Long and thin he was, with big hands and feet jutting out. His buckskin breeches were always too short and too tight, and made blue circles on his legs where they squeezed him. "I can always wash your muddy footsteps from the floor," teased his step-mother, "but keep your head clean, Abe, so you won't be leaving tracks along my whitewashed ceiling." Abe grinned, scratched his head, and thought of a joke. When his stepmother went out for a while he took a little boy with muddy feet, lifted him up and walked him like a fly across the ceiling. "Abe, I should thrash you," said the stepmother when she came back. But she laughed at the joke instead. And with a pail of whitewash Abe made the ceiling white and clean again.

Often for days at a time Abe stayed alone in the woods chopping timber. It was so quiet in the forest, and he had plenty of time to think and dream. At mealtimes he shared his food with the squirrels, and in return they had to listen to the speeches he made up. The squirrels blinked their small brown eyes, and the trees seemed to sway and bow in agreement with what he said. He made a poem for his sister Sally, and when she married and left home, he read it at her wedding.

Abe also left home for a while to be a ferryman on the Ohio River. The great Ohio River flowed by some miles from Little Pigeon Creek, and it was there that he made his first dollar. Two elegant travelers gave him a shiny half dollar each for rowing them out to the steamboat that lay anchored in midstream. But as he stood there in his ferryboat, wondering that anyone could pay so much for so little work, one of the coins slipped out from between his fingers. Sadly Abe saw half of his new wealth vanish in the depths.

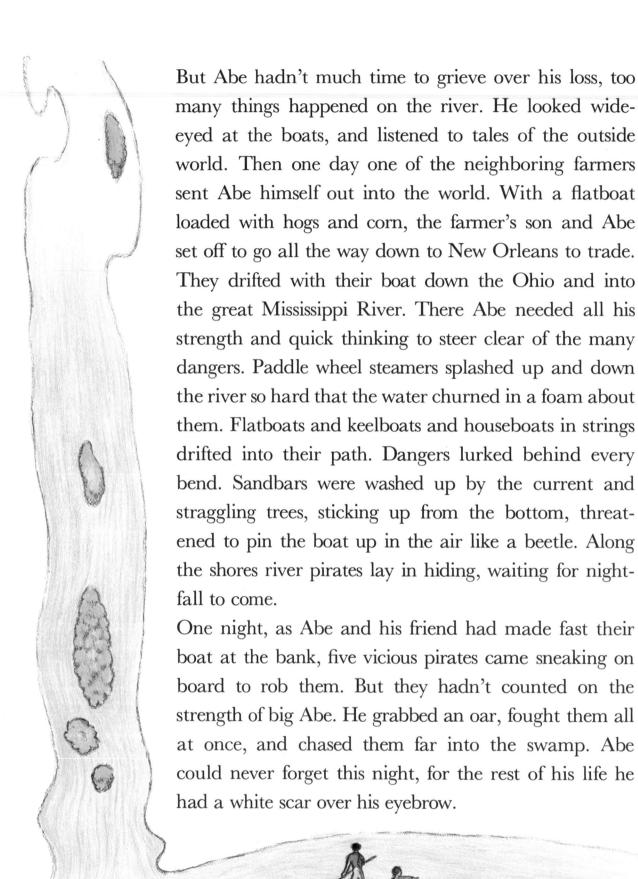

But Abe hadn't much time to grieve over his loss, too many things happened on the river. He looked wide-eyed at the boats, and listened to tales of the outside world. Then one day one of the neighboring farmers sent Abe himself out into the world. With a flatboat loaded with hogs and corn, the farmer's son and Abe set off to go all the way down to New Orleans to trade. They drifted with their boat down the Ohio and into the great Mississippi River. There Abe needed all his strength and quick thinking to steer clear of the many dangers. Paddle wheel steamers splashed up and down the river so hard that the water churned in a foam about them. Flatboats and keelboats and houseboats in strings drifted into their path. Dangers lurked behind every bend. Sandbars were washed up by the current and straggling trees, sticking up from the bottom, threatened to pin the boat up in the air like a beetle. Along the shores river pirates lay in hiding, waiting for night-fall to come.

One night, as Abe and his friend had made fast their boat at the bank, five vicious pirates came sneaking on board to rob them. But they hadn't counted on the strength of big Abe. He grabbed an oar, fought them all at once, and chased them far into the swamp. Abe could never forget this night, for the rest of his life he had a white scar over his eyebrow.

The further south they drifted the more Negro slaves they saw working in the cotton fields. And when, at last, they came to New Orleans, there were black slaves everywhere. Some were running about with loads on their heads, others were led in chains through the streets to be sold at slave markets. And Abe saw how Negroes were trotted up and down like horses to show that they were strong and healthy. The Negro mothers were

weeping, for they never knew if they would ever see their little black babies again when they were sold. Sometimes the one who bought the mother would refuse to take the children, and then they would be sold to someone else and the family would be broken up.

Abe Lincoln thought that was cruel. And when the cargo and the flatboat were sold, he was glad to go north again to his Indiana home where everyone was free.

There all the neighbors came to hear him tell of his adventures out in the big world. They never tired of hearing about the river pirates and slave markets. And they all grinned broadly when he told of the fortune teller who had said that he, Abraham Lincoln, would one day be President of the United States.

Abe's father was listening to stories about Illinois, the new prairie state, where folks said the grass grew greener than anywhere else.

"I reckon we'll be moving on," he said one day. So one early spring morning the Lincolns set off again, this time in a wagon so huge that a seven yoke ox team had to pull it. The wagon was crowded, for many relatives moved with them. They traveled on for two whole weeks through forests and swamps and rolling prairie. On long legs Abe walked in front to peddle pins and buttons, when once in awhile they passed a farm. When they came to the Sangamon River in Illinois they liked the land, and put up a cabin. Abe split mountains of rails for fences. One thousand rails he split for a neighbor to get himself a pair of jeans. That was much work for a pair of pants, but then his legs were long, too, so it took many yards of cloth to cover them. And when spring came he said good-bye to his father and his stepmother, put his belongings into a bundle, threw it over his shoulder, and set out into the world to try his luck. For now he had reached twenty-one years, and was free to do as he pleased.

A little further down the Sangamon River lay the village of New Salem. It had only a few dozen houses, but even Chicago did not have more at that time. There were several stores in New Salem, and a man named Offut was planning to open a new one. On one of his trips up the river Offut met tall Abe, and hired him as clerk in the store he was going to open.

But first he sent him down to New Orleans with goods to sell. Abe built a flatboat himself, and drifted down the Sangamon River. But off New Salem a miller had built a dam across the river, and on this milldam the flatboat stuck. All the people of the village stood on the bank and waited to see the flatboat sink. But Abe bored a hole in the boat and tipped it so the water could flow out, and slowly the flatboat slid over the dam. Then he put a wedge in the hole, and drifted on down the river. There was a mighty smart fellow, everyone said.

Offut went around bragging and betting that his huge new clerk was not only smart enough to outwit them all, but so strong that he could outrun, outjump, and outfight any man in the county. So when Abe came back to New Salem all the strong boys were strutting about like cocks, eager to measure their strength against his. And Abe had to make good Offut's words. He wrestled with the strongest and toughest of them all, and threw them to the ground. Then the beaten boy and all the people cheered and said Abe was the strongest man in the county. From that day they accepted him as one of them. They loved his funny ways and jokes. And they nicknamed him Honest Abe. Once he charged a woman six and a quarter cents too much, and he walked three miles to catch up with her and pay her back.

But Abe's honesty wasn't enough to keep Offut's store going. The debts grew bigger and bigger, and one morning Offut was gone. There stood Abe without a job. But just then the men of New Salem were called to war, for an Indian chief, Black Hawk, had come back to Illinois with his warriors. His tribe had sold the land to the "paleface," but Black Hawk said: "Man-ee-do, the great spirit, gave us the land, it couldn't be sold." "Sold is sold," said the people of Illinois, and went to war to chase the Indians out.

Abe Lincoln went to war as a captain. For the man from each village who had the longest row of men lined up behind him was elected captain. And twice as many men lined up behind Abe as behind his rival.

But his soldiers had never taken orders from any man before, and Captain Abe Lincoln struggled hard to make them obey him. That was all the fighting he had. For Black Hawk and his warriors fled before the soldiers. One day a peaceful old Indian came walking into camp. The soldiers were angry and wanted to kill him, but Abe said, "Anyone who touches him must fight me first." Because Abe was the strongest, they had to obey.

Soon after that Black Hawk was taken prisoner, and The Indian War was over.

Abe went back to New Salem, and he and another young man named Berry decided to open a store of their own. Both were poor, but Abe's word was good as gold, so they borrowed the money, bought the goods, and started to trade. Very soon Abe's friends were saying he was too clever to stand behind the counter all day long. He should go around making speeches so the people would elect him to go to the capital of Illinois.

Abe thought this a very good idea. So he began going about making speeches and joking with the people. When he had mounted a tree stump he started: "I am humble Abraham Lincoln." And the people liked what he said and his funny ways, and they elected him. Every spring he went to the capital. The rest of the year he took care of his store; but all the time he wanted to study to become a lawyer. And it happened that one day as he was

standing in his store, a covered wagon stopped at the door and a stranger came in with a barrel of old stuff he wanted to sell. Abe had no need of the barrel, but he bought it for half a dollar to help the man. And when he opened the barrel he found at the bottom the book he needed to study law. From then on Abe lay most of the time on the counter and studied the book. And the schoolmaster helped him with grammar and English.

In the meantime Berry took care of the store. But instead of selling the goods, he ate and drank the whole day long, and at last he died. There was Abe with all the debts. It was more than a thousand dollars he owed. His store was taken away from him, and all that he owned was sold at an auction.

Abe's father had taught him: "If you make a bad bargain, hug it all the tighter." So instead of running away Abe stayed and toiled to pay back all the debts.

His friends believed in him, and most of all a girl, whose name was Ann Rutledge. She was sure he would become a great man some day, if he would just go on with his studies. And then they would be married, and be happy ever after.

But one day Ann Rutledge took sick and nothing could be done to save her life. From that day on it was as if there were two Abes. The one was gay and full of funny stories, the other was so sad and sorrowful that no one dared to approach him. But he did his work and finished his studies, and one morning he took leave of his friends in New Salem. He borrowed a horse, and sad and penniless he rode off to Springfield, the capital of Illinois, to become a lawyer.

In Springfield he hitched up his horse on the main square and went into the store of Joshua Speed to ask the price of bedding. "I have no money, but if I succeed I'll pay you back," he said to Speed. But Speed felt sorry for sad-faced Abe and told him to take his things upstairs and share his own bed for nothing.

From that time on, Joshua Speed was Abe Lincoln's best friend. He took him to the homes of all his elegant friends. And Abe bought himself store clothes, put a stovepipe hat on his head, and by and by the country lad was changed into a well-known lawyer.

From the prairie all around people came to ask his advice, for they knew he would be fair and square. And the people in Springfield began to say that the two cleverest men in town were awkward Abraham Lincoln and stylish Judge Douglas. The one was fat and small, the other was lean and tall. And they both courted Mary Todd, a lady from Kentucky. She was dainty and witty, with a tongue so sharp that few people but Abe could tongue-tie her.

Little Miss Todd liked the tall Abe Lincoln, but she liked Judge Douglas too. He was elegant and important and Mary was as proud as she was witty. She had great plans for her future.

"The man I am going to marry will be president of the country," she said.

It took her a long while to make up her mind which one of her suitors to choose, for they were both very clever men. At last she chose Abe, and they were married. They did not have much to begin with, for Abe had debts which he had to pay back. But Mary saved and helped him. They paid off the debts, then they bought a house of their own. It was different from Abe's old home. It was painted white and had green shutters. There were many rooms with stylish furniture, lacy curtains, and plushy carpets.

In a few years they had three noisy little boys, who crawled all over long Abe when he lay reading on the soft carpet in the parlor.

His wife did not like him to lie on the floor, nor to open the door himself when the doorbell rang. Those were wilderness manners, she said. He should sit on a chair when he read and send the maid to the door. For now he was an important man; all over Illinois, people were talking about what a clever and honest man he was.

But it wasn't easy for anyone to change the ways of Abraham Lincoln. He milked his own cow, tended his horse, and was a friend of all the children in town. He was never too tired or busy to play and to joke with them.

One evening some of his little friends tied a string across the street, so high up that everyone in town could pass under it but tall Abe Lincoln with his stove-pipe hat. Off flew the hat, and papers scattered in all directions. For instead of using a bag, Abe always stuffed his tall hat with bills and notes and important papers. While Abe stooped to gather them the boys ran out from their hiding places and threw themselves upon him. Abe never lost his temper with them. He laughed at their pranks. He had been full of pranks himself when he was little.

Many months each year Abe spent driving from courthouse to courthouse out on the prairie. One evening, as he drove along a one-track prairie road, huddled up in his shawl, he met a husky fellow in a buggy. They both knew that the one who pulled aside risked getting stuck in the mud.

"Give way," cried Abe.

"Give way yourself," cried the other man.

Slowly Abe rose from his seat. "I'll tell you what I'll do if you don't give way," he shouted in a terrible voice.

And he rose higher and higher, till he looked like a giant against the setting sun.

"Don't grow any higher," pleaded the husky fellow, and drove right into the mud.

As Abe drove by, the man asked in a timid voice:

"What is it you would have done?"

"I would have given way myself," chuckled Abe as he helped the man.

The stranger laughed—as the whole prairie laughed—even the judges had to laugh when Abe joked.

"Abe, you can even make a cat laugh," everyone said.

The years passed and people began to call him Old Abe. He still did not change. When the people of Illinois sent him to Congress, he walked up Capitol Hill in Washington with his pack of books in a red handkerchief slung over his shoulder. He was himself and did not care or even notice if people smiled. After his term in Congress was over he came home again to Springfield and hitched his horse to his buggy as before and rattled out over the prairie to faraway courthouses. There he sat with his feet on the table and seemed to be asleep. But when his turn came he stretched himself into shape, ruffled his hair and took off his coat and necktie. Then he began to speak, and everyone listened. There wasn't a man on the wide prairie who hadn't heard of Old Abe.

For fifteen years Abe Lincoln was too busy as a lawyer to have time for politics. It seemed as if Mary after all hadn't married a man who would be president. It was Judge Douglas who had become a great politician.

All this time there was a great quarrel between the States of the South and the States of the North.

"It is wrong to have slaves," said the Northerners; "let the black slaves go."

"Slaves they are and slaves they shall remain!" cried the Southerners, and they talked of leaving the United States and running their part of the country alone.

Judge Douglas traveled through Illinois making speeches. He said: "Let each state decide for itself whether it wants slavery or not." This aroused Abraham Lincoln. He stood up and said: "All men are created free and equal." There must be the same freedom in all of the United States, he felt, for "a house divided against itself cannot stand." And wherever Douglas made a speech, Lincoln made a speech against what he said.

From afar people came over dusty roads to hear the two best talkers of the state. Judge Douglas was elected senator from Illinois, but Old Abe's fame spread all over the United States.

Everywhere people began to wonder if Lincoln wasn't the man to keep the United States together. From the big towns in the East important men traveled to see him and asked if he would be willing to let the people vote for him as President. Abraham Lincoln thought it over for a long time. It was so friendly and peaceful on the prairie in Illinois.

But all over the North people cried: "We want Honest Old Abe." And at last he said yes.

Late one evening Lincoln got the message that he had been elected President of the United States. He went home to his wife, and said: "Mary, we are elected."

And Mary rejoiced. Her dream had come true.

Abe sold his horse and buggy and cow, and made ready to leave his home. And he grew a beard on his chin. He knew he wasn't handsome, and he thought a beard might make him look nicer.

On a drizzling morning he tied up his trunks. Then he went to the train at the station. He looked at the dear and homey faces of his prairie friends who had come to bid him good-bye. He was sad that he had to go, but the people of his country had called him.

"I bid you all an affectionate farewell," said Lincoln.

"Farewell, farewell," cried all his friends.

And with his wife and his boys Abraham Lincoln traveled to the White House in Washington.

Now Abraham Lincoln was master of the White House. But he was President of only part of the United States. For the Southern States had taken down the Star-Spangled Banner and raised the flag of the Confederacy in its stead. Sad and silent, Lincoln gazed through his spyglass at the Confederate flag that fluttered in the wind on the other side of the Potomac River in Virginia. He pondered how to get the Southern States

back into the Union. He needed quiet to think what to do. But from morning till night the White House was crowded with people seeking his help. Lincoln wanted to listen to them all, but the days were too short. He grew haggard and careworn, and scarcely had time to eat and to sleep. His servants at last put up a screen across the hall so Lincoln could pass unseen. But he was so tall that the top of his head showed above

the screen when he tiptoed from room to room, and so gave him away to the visitors. Then he locked himself in his office with the men in the Cabinet, who were helping him with the government. No man ever loved peace more than Abraham Lincoln. But he firmly believed that his country could be great and strong only as long as all the states were united as one country. The Union must be saved.

With a heavy heart Lincoln called soldiers from the Northern States and sent them to war against the Southerners to force them back into the Union.

The Civil War had begun.

At first his generals and the men in his Cabinet all thought they were much wiser than Abraham Lincoln who came from the wilderness. Lincoln just let them think so. He listened politely to their advices, but he did what he felt was best for the people. "Have you heard the story of the monkey who wanted a longer tail?" he said to his generals, when they asked for ever more honor and power.

"Once upon a time there was a tribe of monkeys that was going to war. The biggest and strongest of them was made their leader. But he didn't think his tail was grand and long enough. If he was to lead them to victory his tail must be longer, he said. And so the monkeys be-

gan to add to it with pieces of tail. But the longer they made it, the longer tail the monkey chief wanted. The tail became longer and longer—in scrolls and coils it lay all over the floor. At last it grew so long that it filled the room clear to the ceiling, and there sat the monkey leader, so entangled in tail that he couldn't move any more."

Thus everyone would fare, who wanted too much, meant President Lincoln.

The soldiers all loved their long, gangling President and his little son, Tad, who often rode at his side. For Mrs. Lincoln used to send Tad along with his father to make him take better care of himself.

Lincoln was father and friend to all the soldiers. They could go to him with their troubles, and he was never too busy to tell a story or laugh at a joke. One day when he was reviewing the troops, one of the generals gave him a wild horse to ride. But Abe Lincoln was an old ranger who knew how to keep in the saddle. He raced up and down the field, without even losing his hat. And the soldiers cheered till they were hoarse.

"We are coming, Father Abraham, four hundred thousand strong," they answered from all the Northern States, when Lincoln called for more soldiers.

And Lincoln helped them and grieved over those that fell on the battlefields as though they were his own sons. It was in memory of those men who had fallen at Gettysburg that he made his most famous speech, the Gettysburg Address.

He tried to make friends with the Southern States, and offered to buy the slaves' freedom, instead of using the money for war. But the South wouldn't listen to him. So on New Year's Day in 1863 Lincoln solemnly signed a paper that made the slaves free forever. It was called the Emancipation Proclamation.

The Southerners fought on, although they had less and less to eat, and had hardly any shoes to put on their feet. For several years Lincoln sought all over the North for a general who could end the war. At last he found General Grant. He was straightforward and brave, and did not waste his time just talking and writing.

"Can you make an end to the war," asked Lincoln.

"If you give me soldiers enough I will," said Grant.

Once more Lincoln called for soldiers, and again men came from all over the North. And Grant did as he had promised. He forced the Southern soldiers out of Richmond, the capital of the Confederacy. Four years after the Civil War had begun the Star-Spangled Banner waved over Virginia again.

The next day President Lincoln walked into the town, holding little Tad by the hand. An old Negro recognized the long, thin man with the tall stove-pipe hat. "Here is our saviour," he cried, and threw himself at Lincoln's feet. And suddenly Lincoln was surrounded by Negroes, weeping and rejoicing as they cried: "Glory, glory hallelujah."

The Civil War had come to an end. The slaves were free, and the Union was saved. Most people in the Northern States wanted to make the Southerners pay for the four terrible years of war. But Lincoln said they should be received back into the Union "with malice towards none, with charity to all." He felt like the father of a great flock of children. Some had run away, but were now returning to their home. He stood on a balcony of the White House, looking out over the cheering people who cried: "Speak, Father Abraham." Abraham Lincoln didn't answer with words. But he made the band play "Dixie," the favorite song of the Southerners, which had not been heard in Washington since the Civil War began. Then he sat down on his rocking chair to rest.

He had done what he should do. He had held together the great nation brought forth upon this continent by his forefathers.

TO WASHINGTON

INDIANA

LITTLE PIGEON CREEK

OHIO RIVER

KENTUCKY

I & E. P. d'AULAIRE

THE ADVENTURES OF US

Getting to Know Guion Bluford Jr.

TIERRA HAYNES

To my husband Dre and my little loves Dre Jr, Devon, and Dallas. Every good thing starts with you.
-Tierra

About Guion Bluford Jr.

Guion Bluford Jr., also known as Guy, was born in Philadelphia, Pennsylvania, in 1942. Guion was a decorated Air Force pilot in Vietnam before joining NASA in the late 1970s. In 1983, he became the first African American to travel into space, where he served as a mission specialist aboard the Challenger. By the time he retired in 1993, Bluford had completed three more NASA missions and compiled more than 688 hours in space.

Among the 10,000+ applicants to the National Aeronautics and Space Administration's (NASA) space program, Guion Bluford Jr. was one of 35 chosen to join the new space shuttle team in January of 1978. He officially became a NASA astronaut in August of 1979. Bluford made history on August 30, 1983, when he became the first African American to experience space travel.

One afternoon, Dre, Devon, and Dallas were waiting for their mom to make lunch.

"Mom, we're so hungry! Is lunch ready yet?!" Devon asked.

"Lunch will be ready soon, boys!" Mom said.

"Let's play video games until it's time to eat," Dre suggested.

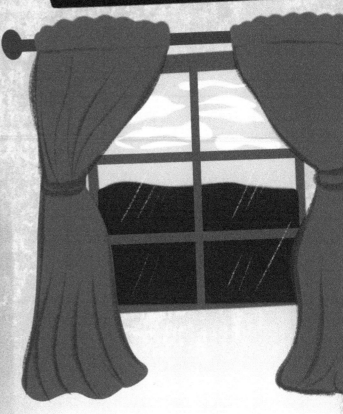

"Let's give the video games a break," Dad said. "Play outside, guys! It's a beautiful day. Enjoy some fresh air."

"Please, Dad!" the boys pleaded in unison.

"This isn't up for debate. Go outside and play. Have fun," Dad instructed as the boys trudged outside.

"What should we do?" Dre wondered aloud. "I know!" he finally said. "Let's play basketball!"

"How about we jump on the trampoline?" Devon suggested.

"I want to play astronauts," Dallas said.

"Dallas, why do you always want to play astronauts?" asked Devon.

"Because when I grow up, I want to be just like my favorite astronaut, Guion Bluford, Jr.!" replied Dallas.

"You want to be like WHO?! Who is Guion Bluford Jr?" Devon and Dre asked in confusion.

"You guys don't listen to Mom at all. She taught us all about him! Guion Bluford Jr. was the first African American to travel into space, and he served as a mission specialist aboard the Challenger. You know, the famous space shuttle? He's my hero!" said Dallas.

"Oh, I kind of remember that! Wasn't Guion an Air Force pilot in Vietnam, too?

Dallas nodded with excitement. "Yup, that's him!"

"Guys, let's play Rock Paper Scissors. The winner gets to pick what we do," Dre suggested.

The three boys bunched up their hands, ready to play. Dallas won, as his rock crushed his brothers' scissors.

"I win!" Dallas cheered. "Grab your helmets, guys. We're going into outer space!"

Dragging their feet, Dre and Devon grabbed their "helmets," picking up cardboard boxes to place on their heads.

"I'm going to be an astronaut someday," Dallas smiled.

"Are you sure about that?" Devon asked.

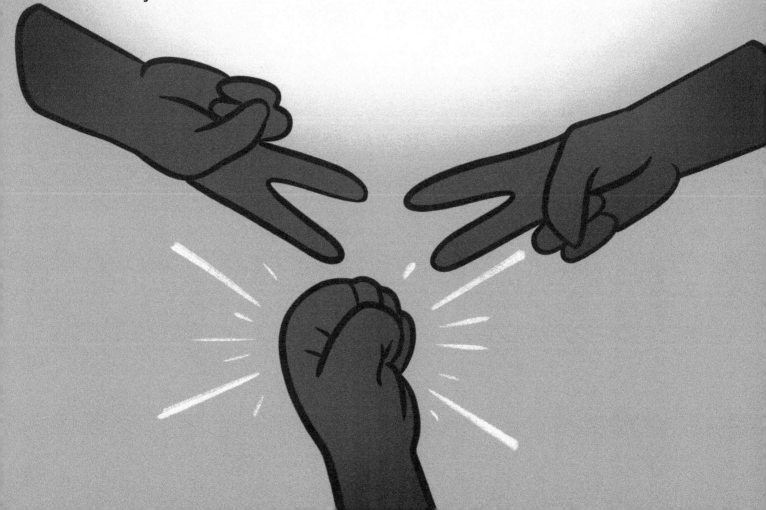

"For sure!" Dallas said. "Just watch. Three… two… one… blastoff!"

Within seconds, the three boys blasted off into outer space.

Dre, Devon, and Dallas landed on the moon and looked around in amazement. Now dressed in full spacesuits and official astronaut helmets, the boys were prepared and ready to explore.

"See? Aren't you guys glad we came to the moon? This is so cool!" Dallas cheered.

"This is beyond cool," Dre happily agreed. "We're walking on the moon!" he said as he bounced around. "I never imagined doing something like this!"

"Hello! You three must be our new class of recruits," a man said, appearing from behind a crater.

"Yup, that's us! But wait, aren't you…Guion Bluford Jr?!" Dallas asked in amazement.

"That's right! But you can call me Guy. Today, I'll be teaching you everything you need to know to become an astronaut. Let's get to work and begin your official astronaut training," Guion said as he led the boys to the training center.

Dallas was in awe of Guion. "I can't believe we're training with Guion Bulford, Jr.," Dallas whispered to Dre. "He's a legend! He's been inducted into the International Space Hall of Fame, the U.S. Astronaut Hall of Fame, and the National Aviation Hall of Fame. He's like the Michael Jordan of astronauts!"

Guion chuckled modestly. "Thank you for that glowing introduction, Dallas. Becoming an astronaut takes a lot of hard work and dedication, but if you put your minds to it, you three can achieve anything," Guion said.

"For example, to prepare for my first night launch, we had to switch our circadian rhythm," Guion explained.

"What's circadian rhythm?" Dre asked.

"It means we had to get used to sleeping in the day and being up at night," Guion explained.

"But why?" Devon chimed in.

"Well, during the night of our launch, we had to wake up at 10 o'clock. We ate breakfast and suited up. Sleeping during the day and staying up at night guaranteed our bodies were prepared to be alert and aware during the shuttle mission. We put our minds to it, and we went for it, even though the adjustment was kind of weird!"

Guion began training the boys, teaching them challenging astronaut duties such as spacewalking and operating the space system. Dallas began to struggle with learning to operate the space system, and he started to become frustrated. He threw his arms in the air, ready to quit.

"C'mon, Dallas. You can do it! You've got this!" Devon and Dre encouraged.

"No, I can't do this!" Dallas cried. "Being an astronaut is too hard. Who was I kidding? I'll never be able to spacewalk. I should just quit so I don't keep embarrassing myself."

"Dallas, we won't let you quit," Dre said, putting his hand on his brother's shoulder. We're brothers, and we're going to stick together to get this done. What's our family motto?"

"Even through fear, we persevere!" the boys shouted in unison.

"You're right, guys. Thanks for reminding me to believe in myself. Let's do this!" Dallas said as he perked up and rejoined training.

The boys finished their astronaut training, and Guion rewarded their hard work and determination with a badge of completion.

"I'm so proud of you," Guion said, "and you should be proud of yourselves, too! It's always great to see a group complete their training, but it's even better to see you work together to succeed. Brothers are your first best friends, and even though you won't always get along, you should always stick together. After all, look at what you've accomplished today."

"I have to admit, I thought training to become an astronaut would be too challenging, and even though it was hard, this showed me I could do anything. I'm so glad we did this together," Dre said, grinning from ear to ear.

"When we work together, we can do anything!" Devon exclaimed.

"That's right!" Guion agreed. "Being an astronaut is extremely hard work, but don't ever let difficulties discourage you from trying."

"Being an astronaut has given me a new appreciation for the Earth. Our planet is a small ball in a large universe. I didn't recognize that until I saw the Earth from afar. Being an astronaut is a labor of love, and once you travel two million miles into space, you want to stay up there forever!" Guion added.

"What was it like when the spaceship took off? Was it scary?' Devon asked.

"It felt exactly like these simulators, except you're really moving! I laughed all the way up! It was such a fun ride. We flew into orbit upside down. It was spectacular," Guion explained.

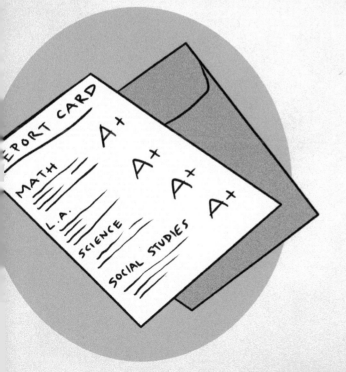

The boys listened in amazement, hanging on to every word of Guion's cool story.

"Thank you for teaching us how to be astronauts. I can't wait to come back!" Dallas said.

"Never stop using your imagination," Guion instructed. "There are so many things you can do to continue your work as astronauts – build airplanes, do crosswords and puzzles, and, of course, the most important thing is to earn good grades in school."

"Mom and Dad always tell us to study hard. I guess they were right!" Devon said.

The boys arrived home safely, planting their feet on the ground and looking around at their house. They gave each other a high five, feeling overjoyed about their awesome experience in outer space.

"Hi, boys!" Mom said as she approached her three sons. "Dallas, your shoe is untied," Mom said, pointing at his laces.

Dallas leaned down to tie his shoe but struggled to finish. Instead of quitting, he looked at his mom and said, "I won't let difficulties discourage me from trying!"

"That's a great lesson, Dallas!" Dad happily exclaimed in surprise.

Dallas smiled. "I learned it from my astronaut training today," he said, walking off to join his brothers on the trampoline.

"Astronaut training...?" Mom confusedly wondered, shrugging her shoulders.

POSITIVE AFFIRMATIONS
FOR BOYS

I AM A KING

I AM LOVED

I AM STRONG

I MATTER

I AM A LEADER

I AM ENOUGH

I AM FEARLESS

I AM BLESSED

I AM UNSTOPPABLE

I AM KIND

I AM PROUD

I AM JOY

MEET THE AUTHOR

Tierra Haynes, author of *The Adventures of Us*, was born in Euclid, Ohio, and now resides in Maryland with her loving husband and three wonderful sons. As a rising author, Tierra looks forward to unveiling more books within this magical series, books that follow the Haynes boys as they learn more about African American history through imagination and play. Between motherhood, entrepreneurial endeavors, writing, and life, Tierra enjoys watching football (Go Browns!), trips to Target, and her self-care love language of taking vacations. Tierra is a proud graduate of Kent State University, earning a Bachelor of Arts degree in communications, yet remains in the mind frame of a student, welcoming every opportunity to learn and grow. To connect with Tierra, please visit www.mommyonthemove.info, and be sure to tune into her highly acclaimed podcast, Mommy on the Move, available on Apple, Spotify, and Anchor.

FOLLOW US

@mommyonthemove

www.facebook.com/IAmMommyOnTheMove

MOMMY ON THE MOVE

www.mommyonthemove.info

CPSIA information can be obtained
at www.ICGtesting.com
Printed in the USA
LVHW071324250421
685380LV00001B/1